DEDICATION

For my beloved Grandmothers, Grandma Perry, and Grandma Brown, I'm sorry it took me so long to get this done.

ACKNOWLEDGEMENT

Thank you to my three youngest daughters who ground me and keep me focused on why I get up every morning. I don't know where I would be if you three had not come along when you did. It's been a wild ride, and we've been through a lot together, but please know that you are my heart.
Thank you to my oldest daughter who taught me what it was to be a mom. For being my first best friend, and my first true heartbreak. You have inspired so much of what I write.
Thank you to my son, who I see so much of myself in. I don't have the words to express how special you are. You are wise beyond your years, and more incredible than you realize.
Thank you to my grandparents who loved me from the moment I was born and believed in me even when I didn't believe in myself.
Thank you to Tiffany for being the best girlfriend a girl could want and need.
Thank you to Marcus, for showing me what love is and what love isn't

Beyond the Obvious

Jennifer Brown-Carrillo

BookLeaf
Publishing

Presentation by *BookLeaf Publishing*

Web: www.bookleafpub.com

E-mail: info@bookleafpub.com

ISBN: 9789357211987

First edition 2023

PREFACE

Life is not easy, but it is beautiful. I have had more than my fair share of pain, but I have also had more than my fair share of beautiful moments. I chose to turn my tragedy into triumph, and rather than get stuck in the madness, I turned the fear into fuel. I refused to listen to those who said I would never accomplish anything and did the impossible anyway.

North Star

Let me be your north star, in a world of chaos
and confusion.
Let me be your north star, your starting and your
ending points, so you can always find your way
home.
Let me be your north star, a reminder that you
always have a place that you belong, a place
where you are loved.
Let me be your north star, when life is unkind, or
you feel overwhelmed.
Let me be your north star, your point A, when
you get lost getting to point B
Let me be your north star.

True Heartbreak

They say that heartbreak comes from loving a lover
I say that heartbreak comes from loving a child
Watching them make decisions that you know aren't good them
Wanting to intercede on their behalf, to prevent them from getting hurt
But knowing that they have to learn for themselves
Having your heart ripped out when they scream
"I hate you" when things don't go their way, and they blame you
Yes, heartbreak does not come from loving a lover
True heartbreak comes from being a mother

Battered

I used to dream of bright spaces, happy faces,
colorful places
I saw the world with eyes wide shut
Believing that the world was mine for the taking
I could do anything, be anyone, I was going to
take the world by storm
Then I met you and you darkened my dreams
You stole my innocence, shattered my illusions,
drained my hope
You battered my spirit, my mind, and my body
Instead of dreaming of bright spaces, happy
faces, and colorful places, I now have
nightmares
Cold, dark empty spaces, twisted distorted
faces, and places devoid of color
I no longer see the world with eyes wide shut,
my eyes are too swollen to see anything at all
The world is no longer mine for the taking, you
have taken everything from me
Where I once believed I could be anyone, do
anything, I know now I was foolish

Treasure Them Always

Treasure them Always.
Little girls grow up faster than you realize.
Always remember they have their own voice
that needs to be heard.
Promise me that you will listen, really listen.
Validate their feelings.
Even if you don't agree
Promise to never give up, even when they fight
back, and you feel hope is lost.
Hold tight to the first moment you held them in
your arms and looked into their eyes
That will be the feeling that helps you get
through the dark nights.
Remember that feeling of pure love and
euphoria when they are the ones breaking your
heart.
Engage with them daily.
On the big things, on the little things.
Listen and really hear them when they speak
Notice when they don't
Pay attention to the lyrics of their favorite song,
What are they trying to tell you?
Always ask them how their day was, and be
ready to listen

Learn to pick up on the subtle cues that it wasn't a good day
Never pressure them into talking before they are ready, but make sure they know they can always come to you.
If you promise you won't get mad, then don't
Remember, words once spoken, can't be taken back
Tell them that they are beautiful, they need to know this
But more important than that
Tell them that they are smart, and brave, confident, and strong
Capable and can do anything they set their mind to
Encourage them to follow their dreams
To have wild, grand adventures, to follow their hearts, and live big full lives
Remember, that you are here to help guide them, but ultimately this is their path, and they must choose which path to walk
Love them, even when you don't like them
Celebrate the little things, this will reinforce that you care
When you are overwhelmed, and you will be, remember, it's not their fault, they're overwhelmed too.
My sweet girl, who gave the sweetest gift, treasure this time, because in a blink of an eye,

you'll be looking at your girls raising their girls,
and writing to them
"Treasure them always…."

Thank you

Thank you
You tried to break me
You told me I would never accomplish anything
without you
That I was nothing
I was a failure
I believed you for a time
One day I stopped believing your lies
I picked myself up off the dusty floor of
self-doubt and misery
Cleaned the cobwebs out of my mind
I took back my life
Rebuilt it brick by brick
Now I have a career
I own a house
And you?
Turned out, you were nothing without me
Thank you
Your words were fuel for my fire

Stranger in the Mirror

Day by day my reflection changed until the
person in the mirror became a stranger
No rhyme, no reason, my hair was falling and
there was no stopping it
My blue eyes stared back, but I didn't recognize
them
Who was this person staring back at me
Beauty is in the eye of the beholder, but I didn't
feel beautiful
No eyebrows
No eyelashes
No hair
I had to learn to love myself again
Slowly, day by day
Bald is beautiful
What a thing to say
Then one day I believed it, I found confidence in
it
I took my power back
The stranger in the mirror became the person I
love to see
She is strong
She is me

I loved you

I loved you from the moment I saw you
I saw home in your eyes
Felt safe in your arms
Our souls connected, and I experienced a love like I had never known
I was walking on clouds, my head in the rainbows
You were the one I would spend my life with, I was certain
I loved you more than I had ever loved anyone
More than I thought possible
I let down my walls
I let you in
I told you my secrets
Shared my dreams
I would look at you and smile, so sure you were my happily ever after
I loved you fiercely
I only wanted to be with you forever
Falling asleep listening to your heartbeat was my favorite part of the day
Waking up and seeing you next to me started my day with a smile
Nothing could go wrong as long as you were by my side

I loved you
I loved you more than I loved myself
I lost myself in you
I didn’t care, as long as I had you, I didn’t care
I care now, because you are gone, and I am lost
Lost in the memories of who I used to be
Strong, independent, careful, wise
I’m left with the memories of a time when
I loved you

Scars like Wings

She always seemed to be a bit out of place
Like an old soul in a young body
She never quite fit in with anyone or any place
She felt things deeply or not at all
She was tragically and beautifully broken
She wore her scars like wings, and she soared through life gracefully
Those who she let close enough loved her
Those who believed to know her admired her
Those who knew of her were a bit intimidated by her
She was beauty, grace, courage, and fierceness all wrapped into one
She rolled with the punches, never giving up
When life knocked her down, she always got back up
She believed in love, even if love didn't believe in her
She was magic
In a world that no longer believed in magic
That is what made her so special, she was love, magic, and she never gave up, even when the world gave her every reason why she should.

I left my heart behind

Drip
Drip
Drip
The rain is falling from a heavy sky
I have to say goodbye to you, but I don't know how
I stare at the ground, hearing the rain hit the umbrella, I lower it, I want to die
Drip
Drip
Drip
I watch them lower you into the ground
I want to scream "WAIT!"
"STOP!"
Instead, I stand there silently, tears streaming down my face
Memories of you overwhelming my mind, threatening to drown me and pull me under
I can't believe that you are gone
Drip
Drip
Drip
I walk to the edge and stare at the hole in the ground,

Family and friends are throwing in flowers, I can hear them crying, and wailing
Someone says something to me, but I can't hear what they are saying. I want to be with you
Drip
Drip
Drip
I look at the white rose that I hold in my hand, finally letting it go
I watch as it falls down, landing gently on top of the casket
It's not fair.
Drip
Drip
Drip
I have to say goodbye to you
The only person who ever loved me for me
As I walked away from you that day, I left my heart behind

My Daughter

To my daughter
This world will tell you that you can't because
You are a woman
You are weaker
You are too bossy
You are emotional
You are too sensitive
I'm here to tell you that you can because
You are a woman
You are strong
You were born to lead
You are emotional
You are sensitive
You see, the world needs more kindness
The world needs more compassion and love
When the world tells you that you can't do
something, remember that you can do anything
that you choose to do.
Be fearless, be bold, be kind
Never forget who you are
Always remember that you are loved

Gone

Our eyes met and our souls recognized one another
I had never experienced this feeling before
My heart came alive
I felt calm
Peace
You were the one
So why are you gone?

Tears run dry

There is nothing left to do but say goodbye to you
Your bags are packed, your sunglasses on, your left foot is out the door
I stand back and watch you leave
Wanting to yell for you to stay
Knowing it won't change anything
I hold my head high, forcing a straight face
Refusing to let you see me cry
I watch you leave
The taillights fade away
With them all hope fades away
Now that you are gone, I crumble to the floor
Sobbing
Shaking
Finally allowing myself to feel the pain of losing you
Tears run dry
My head hurts
I pick myself up, smooth my skirt and turn to face reality
You are gone

Moonlight

Moonlight streams through the open window
Our bodies intertwined on the bed
I can feel your heartbeat against mine
Our eyes lock
I have loved you before, in another time, my
soul knew your soul, and when we met in this
life, it was like coming home. I have no doubt
that we will find each other in the next life.
I know I will love you forever. You are it for me.
You're the oxygen I need to breathe
You're the smile on my lips
You broke down my walls and thawed my
frozen heart
You made me believe in love
I miss you when you're not with me
I love you isn't enough to express how I feel
about you.
I adore you
I appreciate you
I celebrate your existence
I cherish you
You are my favorite person
I would be lost without you

Snow

I hate the snow
Not because it's cold
But because it reminds me of you
Snow covered the ground the day I lost you
The day I felt my heart turn to ice
The day I lost myself to the darkness
You were my first love, and oh how I loved you
I stood looking out the window up at the night sky, watching the snow falling, tears streaming down my face
Eventually the tears dried, my eyes swelled shut, and I collapsed onto my bed, sleep would not come
I thought about our time together
Plans we had made
Dreams unfulfilled
How would I live my life without you by my side?
The world seemed darker, larger, scarier.
I hate the snow
Not because it's cold
But because it reminds me of you

My heart

You are my heart
I was lost during our time apart
I couldn't sleep without the light on
as if the dark would make it permanent and you would never come home again
my heart ached in a way that I had never felt before
I cried
Something I am not accustomed to doing
I would be fine one minute, and then the next I was on the floor, sobbing, gasping for air, wondering what in the hell was wrong with me, where were these tears coming from and if they would ever stop.
I would dream of you walking through the door
Telling me that you were home
That it had all been one big mistake
I would go through the motions of my day
Work
Taking care of the kids
Cleaning the house
Nothing made sense without you here
I had never known love like ours before
Maybe that was the problem
Love

It is such a fickle thing
It sure has gotten the better of me

One Thing

If I could say one thing
To the scared little girl who sat alone in the dark
I would tell her I love her
I would tell her that she's brave
I would tell her that she's going to be okay
Despite the fact that she wasn't loved
Despite the fact that she was abused
Broken
Damaged
Nearly destroyed
If I could tell the little girl who grew into an angry teenager who nearly destroyed herself one thing
I would tell her to keep going
To hold her head high when people insulted her
When the world got ugly with her
When she married the man who tried to kill her
I would reassure her that she would survive
She would move on and instead of crumbling
She would build a beautiful life for herself and her children
If I could tell her one thing, I would tell her I love her
I would tell her she turns out to be fierce

She turns out to be everything she dreamt of being and more

More Than a Four-Letter Word

Our legs are intertwined together in the sheets
Our fingers interlocked
My head is resting on your chest
I can hear your heartbeat
The rain is falling against the window
This is where I belong
Tangled up in you
Do you know how much I love you?
I say the words, but somehow, they don't seem
to be enough
You're the air that I breathe
the sun that warms my skin
the food that feeds my soul
the calm that soothes my storms
You're the missing part that I didn't realize I was
missing
So, when I say I love you, know that it is more
than just a four-letter word

Society

Who are you?
Are you who they said you would be?
Who do you see when you look in the mirror?
Are you happy with the person that stares back?
Do you listen when they say you're not good
enough
Not pretty enough
Not thin enough
Not smart enough
Who are you?
Do you realize that it's all societies insecurities
being projected onto you?
Shake it off
Lift your head
You are who you decide to be
You are in control
You get to decide of you are good enough
Pretty enough
Thin enough
Smart enough
You get to decide who you are
Not society

Words like Razors

Do you know how deeply your words cut when you speak?
Like razor blades across my skin
Tearing the flesh from my soul
I think you do; I think you take pleasure from it
Watching the pain appear in my eyes
The tears spill down my cheeks
I think you know exactly how deep your words cut
I think you simply don't care
I can feel myself dying from the inside out
I hate myself for letting you in
I hate myself for allowing you to make me feel this way
I used to be stronger than this
What is wrong with me
Am I being punished for something?
This pain in the pit of my stomach
It's too much to take

Shadows

I realized something today
I no longer recognize the woman in the mirror
She used to be strong
Fierce
Independent
Fearless
Now she is weak, weepy, a mess
I still see a glimmer of her in there, waiting for
me to grab her out of the darkness
Bring her back into the light
Shake off the demons that plague her
The shadows that haunt her
Those that hold her back
It's time to say goodbye to those who hurt her

One day

One day, just like that I no longer needed you
My heart stopped hurting
I no longer cared what you thought
I stopped checking my phone to see if you called
When I woke up in the morning, you were not
the first thought I had
At night, you were not the last person I thought
of before I fell asleep
It didn't hurt when someone said your name or
asked how you were doing, I simply replied with
"I don't know"
But one day hasn't arrived yet
I need you

www.ingramcontent.com/pod-product-compliance
Lightning Source LLC
Chambersburg PA
CBHW051751130826
49812CB00033B/1105
9789357211987